Foreword

The villages Of Ecclefechan, Eaglesfield, Kirtlebridge and Kirkpatrick-Fleming, described in this volume generally owe their existence to the location of the tower houses of the powerful landowners who resided nearby and to the valleys of the Mein and Kirtle Waters. These valleys were a natural route to and from England and had seen the Roman and English armies traverse them at various times.

The area became known as the 'Debatable Lands' due to all the fighting over it between the English and the Scots, and between the Scots themselves. In the late 16th Century the fighting was mainly between the border reivers and clans, with raiding parties crossing back and forth over the border to pillage and burn their enemies' holdings and farms. This resulted in the building of fortified farms and tower houses and in a number of cases the tower house was incorporated or replaced by a later building on or near the site of the earlier one. Villages were strung out along the river valleys generally following the line of the ancient route. In 1820 Thomas Telford was awarded a contract to build a decent road from Carlisle to Glasgow and he employed John Park as his mason for all the local bridgeworks required. Telford's road bypassed some villages and in 1870 the Caledonian Railway line followed suit, although stations were built close by. The railway enabled goods such as pork, lime, sandstone and garments made locally to be exported and goods for the businesses to be brought back, along with coal for heating. The railway stations closed in the 1960s.

Telford's road was upgraded, becoming the A74 in the 1960s and then the M74 came along in the 1990s, bypassing all the villages. As with other areas the day of the large house has passed and shops in the villages have declined. However, tourism is very important to the area and it is also a commuter belt for those who travel to work in Carlisle, Annan, Dumfries and Lockerbie. New housing has also appeared in these villages, bringing young families and breathing new life into the communities.

Right: An elderly couple dressed in their Sunday best outfits; the house in the background is probably Knockburn Lodge of Knockhill Estate, near Hoddom Castle. The contraption the lady is sitting in, perhaps made by the local blacksmith, looks like a novel way of getting around; possibly they were on their way to Hoddom Parish Church some three and a half miles distant. An added safety feature was the oil lamp which can be seen hanging on the back of the handcart.

Looking north up Ecclefechan High Street to the top of the Square about 1910, from a point near to the Royal Bank of Scotland building (marked with an x) which stands behind the ornate cast-iron fountain on the immediate left. Its glass globe light finial is thought locally to have been gifted by the Brooks family of Hoddom Castle and returned to them in the late 1930s. Beyond Bank House can be seen Smithy House, a two-storey villa with its adjoining smithy. The white gabled house now has a single-storey extension and houses a branch of Cost Cutters. Burnbank Road with its small cottages leading up past the Haggs to the station then opens up. The long building on the right is Garthwaite Place, with the shops belonging to Creelman painters and Garthwaite tailors, with the white building beyond an inn. The other road off centre to the right was the Howrigg road (now Hall Road) leading to Kirkconnel Hall and on towards Middlebie. The three-storey building at the junction was a disused cotton mill and was blown up by the army during training in the Second World War. Recent housing now stands on this site.

Old Ecclefechan, Eaglesfield, Kirtlebridge and Kirkpatrick Fleming

Raymond Hood

This 1920s view looks towards the centre of Ecclefechan from the Haggshead area of the village. The road follows the route of Thomas Telford's improved road built in the early 19th Century; it became the A74 in the 1960s and is now designated the B7076. The Haggs was once the common grazing for beasts belonging to villagers and now serves as playing grounds. The road junction on the left is that of Burnbank Street leading down into the Townhead area and the old market square at the top of High Street. In the distance to the right can be seen the Johnstone United Presbyterian Church and the buildings flanking Hoddom Road. In the distant left the roof of the United Free church, built in 1878, stands out. To the left of the car (possibly a Rolls-Royce Silver Ghost) the memorial for Thomas Carlyle would be erected in 1929.

Text © Raymond Hood, 2017.
First published in the United Kingdom, 2017,
by Stenlake Publishing Ltd.
54-58 Mill Square, Catrine, KA5 6RD
01290 551122
www.stenlake.co.uk

ISBN 9781840337938

Printed by
Blissetts, Unit 1, Shield Drive, West Cross Industrial Park, Brentford, TW8 9EX

**The publishers regret that they cannot supply
copies of any pictures featured in this book.**

Acknowledgements

Many thanks to the following people who have shared their memories of the villages: David Cochrane, Ian Gilbert, Freddie Horsburgh, Chris and Claire Irving, Elaine Irving, James Johnstone-Ferguson, Peter Rae, Joanne Strong, George and Betty Young. Thanks also to my brother John and my partner Sandra for all their encouragement and assistance in keeping me focused on this book.

Further Reading

The books listed below were used by the author during his research. None of them are available from Stenlake Publishing. Those interested in finding out more are advised to contact their local bookshop or reference library.

Kirkpatrick Fleming – On the Borders of History, D. & S. Adamson, 2010.
Country Life in Scotland, Alexander Fenton, 2008.
The Industrial Archaeology of Scotland, John R. Hume, 1976.
The Reivers, Alistair Moffat, 2008.

Another view of the High Street, from 1910 and taken slightly north of the previous photograph. Bank House is to the immediate right with Smithy House beyond the whitewashed wall and the front of the single-storey smithy is beyond that. Off centre, the Townhead road, now known as Burnbank Street, leads up past the Haggs to the station. From the early 18th Century the Square was the market place for the surrounding area and monthly markets were held selling all sorts of goods. With the advent of the railway the markets declined and had stopped by 1870. During the construction of the railway in the 1840s Irish and English navvies, who were camped nearby, would come into the village on Fridays to be paid and make a nuisances of themselves with their drinking.

The market square at the top of Ecclefechan High Street, looking south around 1905 with a little girl standing in front of the entrance to Bankside Court. The two-storey Bank House is on the right; manager Thomas Shankland's living quarters were upstairs. The bank is listed in trade directories before 1900 and would have served the traders and farmers for miles around. Beyond the fountain, the premises of J. Tennant, draper and stationer, are visible at the corner of School Road (now Academy Street) along with that of D. Clow, grocer. On the left beyond the cottage can be seen the Globe Inn, the whitewashed Commercial Hotel and the Bush Hotel.

Taken about 1905, this photograph of Ecclefechan High Street looking south shows the Square at its widest point. In the foreground two girls stand over the Ecclefechan Burn, unknown to them as it was covered over at the expense of Dr George Arnott of nearby Kirkconnel Hall. The white building to the immediate left is the Commercial Hotel (proprietor Charles Inglis), with the Bush Hotel (proprietor George Campbell) alongside. The two-storey building beyond that with its distinctive turreted roof housed the premises of John Scott, boot and shoemaker, while set back out of sight was the old post office with cottages beyond (the post office still stands although the cottages have been replaced by flats). On the right are the shops of J. Tennant and D. Clow.

Looking north up Ecclefechan High Street towards Townhead, this view from the 1930s shows a quiet Square with few people to be seen. On the immediate right a man is standing outside John Scott's boot and shoe shop with its turreted roof just in view; it was sometimes called the 'Turret Hoose' by the villagers. The Bush Hotel just beyond is now simply shown as a hotel with its façade painted as is that of the Commercial Hotel next door. This is followed by Globe House which was an inn about 1850 but by 1915 had become a shop, owned by various businesses over the years (nowadays it is a hairdresser's, Alice's Salon). Off centre on the left can be seen the start of Burnbank Street while out of sight to the right is the start of the Howrigg road, now known as Hall Road.

A view of the bottom end of Ecclefechan's Square taken outside the Bank House and showing an early lorry sitting outside the Globe Inn. There are more cars parked outside the Commercial and Bush hotels and on the right John Bell's shop can be seen. Further down High Street the distinctive two-storey Carlyle House is visible on the left with its pillared and pedimented doorway.

A much later view of Ecclefechan Hotel which by 1930 had absorbed both the Commercial and Bush hotels. Dating from 1954, this view could have been taken yesterday if it wasn't for the car. In the early 1800s a coach trip from London to Glasgow took approximately 55 hours and could only be afforded by wealthy people. On Saturday, 16 August 2014, a horse-drawn stagecoach left Edinburgh bound for Gretna Green, taking three days to complete the 80-mile journey with four teams of four horses used in relays. The journey raised funds for Macmillan Support Care and replicated part of the route taken by the mail coaches of the early 1800s which passed through Ecclefechan daily and would have changed horses at the hotel.

Looking down High Street from the top of School Road, the old post office is on the left, a three-bay building with a central door and large windows on either side. It has a slated roof with scrolled skewputts at the gable verges. The photograph dates from about 1910 when the building was occupied by J.A. Anderson, grocer and draper, who also sold Kodak film among other items. It is reputed locally that petrol pumps were situated outside the shop to fuel the post vans. The old post office changed hands several times and became W.A. Thomson's chemist's in 1920. Today the name 'Graham, Drapers' (in business from 1900 to 1911) can still be seen on the door lintel in faded paint. The ivy-clad Carlyle House beyond stands out from the other buildings with its kerbside wall and railings.

In this view looking east towards the Townfoot end of the High Street about 1910, the lady is crossing the road close to the wall in the centre which protects the public and other traffic from falling into the Ecclefechan Burn which emerges from its culvert at this point. Beyond the ducks the Arched House is visible. The single-storey building on the near side of the Arched House contained two homes, one belonging to James Tait, blacksmith, with the smithy behind, and the other to David Halliday, a clogger. The building has been made into one house today and there is an ornate date stone, dated 1749, built into its front wall. The Arched House is thought to have been the Carlyle family residence from the 1780s. Even with the culvert being renewed in the 1970s, this view has hardly changed.

The Arched House, seen here around 1900, was the birthplace of Thomas Carlyle, philosopher, author, satirist, translator and mathematician. The upstairs room to the right with the window box is reputed to have been where he was born in 1795 in a truckle bed. The house was built by his father and his uncle who were builders. On the other side of the arch the door shows a sign for a dairy, with the small window displaying some of its stock. Carlyle was educated locally until the age of thirteen when it was said that he walked 80 miles to Edinburgh to enrol at the university. He went on to teach and translated various works to help with his finances. A three-volume historical work about the French Revolution brought him fame and he and his wife moved to London. Carlyle's wife died in 1866 at their London home and when Carlyle died in 1881 his body was brought back to Ecclefechan for burial. The house was opened to view shortly thereafter and some of his belongings from London are on display in the downstairs room. The house is now looked after by the National Trust for Scotland.

This photograph from about 1910 looks north up Ecclefechan's High Street. On the extreme left is the Arched House. On the right is Carlyle House, the Carlyle family home from 1799. The second two-storey building beyond Carlyle House is the old post office with its distinctive large windows. Beyond that can be seen the rounded frontage of John Scott's shop (he was a boot and shoemaker) and beyond that are the Commercial and Bush hotels fronting onto the square. The only differences today are that modern flats have been built between the old post office and Carlyle House and the two white cottages on the left are now one dwelling. *Inset*: Thomas Carlyle.

Looking up Hoddom Road towards School Road (now Academy Street) and the High Street, this view from the 1920s shows some children standing on the road outside Hartrop cottage to their right with a postman behind them. Beyond that is the Johnstone United Presbyterian Church. Also known as St Fechan's church, it was built in 1866 at a cost of £2,752. It is a T-plan church with a square tower on its north flank and a transverse hall incorporating a church officer's flat. The tower was designed to take clock faces at a future date. The church became the new Hoddom Parish Church after a fire in 1972 burned out the old one. On the left, beyond the junction with Main Street, stands the old village school with its distinctive bell tower and across the road from it is the old police station. The school has now been demolished and replaced at another site by a modern building, although the bell tower has been retained as part of Hoddom Court housing complex. In the 1950s Hartrop cottage housed the village's horse-drawn hearse but is now marked only by the remnants of its front wall while the church is now in private ownership.

This view looks eastwards along Main Street from the School Road junction towards the Bellsland area. The row of cottages in the foreground dated from the mid-19th Century but no longer stands. The church was built in 1878 for a United Free congregation and the first minister was a Rev. William Howie. The two-storey buildings beyond the church backed onto Bellsland, no doubt named after its owner. Further along, a smaller two-storey building housed the Redline garage with the site of the village gas works just out of sight behind the last building, Gas Works cottage. The treasurer and secretary for the Gas Light Co. at this time was Thomas Shankland who also looked after the Royal Bank's business. The Free Church closed in 1912, followed by the gas works in 1934 when electricity came to the village. The Free Church building was converted into a village hall in 1920 and continues to be used today.

VILLAGE FROM EAST, ECCLEFECHAN.

This photograph from about 1903 looking west along Main Street (the original Telford road), as it was then known, allows an early view of the Redline garage, owned by W.B. Stewart. The garage was originally the smithy belonging to John Irving with his house adjoining. The garage was still in existence in the 1940s as the Burnswark Garage. The church is still in use as a village hall with an extension built onto its west side.

CLEUGH BRAE MILL
ECCLEFECHAN

Located north of Ecclefechan just off the Middlebie road (B725), this mill served as both an oatmeal mill and a sawmill. The main mill building on the right probably dates back to the 17th Century and was a three-storey rubble construction with a slate roof. The grain would have been hoisted up to the top floor and fed into hoppers which fed into the stones on the first floor. The gearing from the large overshot wheel would connect to the stones here and then the meal fed into the discharge chutes on the ground floor. The wheel can be seen with its box trestle connecting to the mill lade. The adjoining square building with its pyramidal roof and central chimney stack would have housed the grain store and kiln for drying the grain, venting the moisture out of the central roof ventilator. The building just visible to the extreme right would have housed the sawmill. The buildings just off-centre to the left were storerooms and that on the extreme left was the miller's house. In 1882 it was owned by Walter Little and his son David. David was still in business in 1902 but by the 1950s there was no trace of the mill machinery left and it is now part of a mixed farm owned by the Henderson family. The mill building itself is now derelict and unused.

Middlebie school and schoolhouse were built in 1873 on the westernmost fringe of the hamlet of the same name. A small hamlet of roughly 20 houses, a church and manse, and a village hall, it lies midway between Ecclefechan and Waterbeck with the school serving the local area. The school initially had 28 pupils taught by a Mr William Drummond, but was soon catering for 63 pupils drawn from the surrounding area. As was customary back then it would have taken in pupils up to the age of fourteen years old. Originally it had only one classroom but in 1898 a second one was added. The curriculum would to a great extent depend on the knowledge of their teachers, but reading, writing and arithmetic would have been prominent. The school served the community for almost 100 years and closed in 1972 on the retirement of Mrs D. Gorman, head teacher. The fifteen pupils left on the roll were transferred to nearby Hottsbridge School. The village has doubled in size and has a new community centre and some council houses, and the church is still in use.

Another small hamlet to the north-east of Ecclefechan, Waterbeck consists of Old Waterbeck and New Waterbeck. The village developed in the mid-18th Century when Thomas and Robert Carlyle, distantly related to Thomas Carlyle's family, began breeding pigs and selling their produce. As their business prospered it attracted other trades into the area and also a church to serve the needs of the neighbourhood. In this view of New Waterbeck from the early 1900s James Millar the blacksmith is chatting to a cyclist. The rest of the cyclists are standing at the corner of Carlyle's warehouse. The warehouse was a store for the shop with housing on the top floor. In the middle of the road two gentlemen are looking towards the photographer as are the blacksmith's assistants on the right in front of the smithy. One of the buildings behind the old pump in the foreground housed Latimer's shop. William Latimer was a watchmaker by trade and his wife sold sweets from the same premises. The cottages out of picture on the right housed a clogger's business and home and also the post office until it moved in the late 1960s over to Carlyle's shop. Above the trees can be seen the spire of the United Presbyterian church built in 1869. The warehouse has been demolished and the old stables to its rear converted to housing, as have the old coach house and the church.

Another view of New Waterbeck. On the left, behind the postman, is the shop owned by the Carlyle pig breeders. They exported bacon and cheese to Newcastle amongst other places and imported salt for their business. The largest employers locally, they later branched into dealing in wool and seeds. The wool was exported to Wakefield via steamship from Annan. As the firm prospered so did the village and a shop was opened, selling all goods including luxury items and stationery. To the right of the shop was Waterbeck House with its low wall and railings. The Carlyles' headquarters were latterly at Templehill House whose entrance is just out of picture to the right. Although the founders' great-grandsons died in the First World War, the firm continued and was still trading in the 1970s. The village post office had moved into the shop in the late 1960s and was run by Betty Young into the 1970s when it closed. The Carlyle business was bought by A.T. Simpson, seedsmen, who still operate today from a base on the Whitesands, Dumfries.

Looking north up the Beech-lined Hoddom Road towards Ecclefechan, on the left is the Hoddom Cross smithy with the blacksmith's wife and child at the front door. The smithy was housed in an extension to the rear of the cottage. On the other side of the road stands Hoddom Parish Church which was built in 1817 by John Park, mason. In the 1970s fire consumed the interior and roof and the church was never re-instated, but still stands today as a roofless shell. The smithy is now a private residence.

An assembly of huntsmen, foxhounds and followers at the south west side of Hoddom Castle around 1905. The castle dates back to the 16th Century with additions and extensions being made until the 19th Century. The Dumfriesshire Hunt's black and tan fox-hounds were well known across the border region for their low-scenting powers and their deep baying cry. The origins of the hunt date back to the early 1800s. The Jardine family of Castlemilk House, Lockerbie, were associated with it for a hundred years; in 1895 they were joint masters with the Brooks family who had bought Hoddom Castle in 1877. In the 1930s the castle became a youth hotel and during the Second World War an army training camp was located here. Due to legislation in 2001 which led to membership loss and the aftermath of the foot and mouth outbreak the pack was dispersed, although visiting hunts hunted over available countryside for the next three seasons. In 2006 the hunt was resurrected as the Dumfries and Stewartry Hunt and with careful nurturing of younger pony club members it has seen membership grow and its future now seems assured. One of the current joint masters, Nicky Birkbeck, is a direct descendant of Charles Brooks and the current chairman is Annie Cunningham-Jardine who has a family connection to the Jardines of Castlemilk. Hoddom castle, unoccupied and mainly roofless, is now the focal point of a caravan and camping park.

Kirtlebridge mill, the miller's house and associated buildings, seen here around 1920, lies about one mile south of Kirtlebridge. The building on the left housed the mill and machinery whilst the wheel was housed in the low building to the rear. The long building on the right with the double doors would have housed the cart shed and slightly to the left is the door to the top storey of the granary. The building in the centre was the miller's house. Like the other mills it would have ground corn and a little barley. At this time a David Creighton was listed as the mill owner; later entries in the trades directories mention a Mrs Creighton, possibly his widow, as a miller but without naming the mill. The mill's lade from the Kirtle Water was thought to run alongside the fence shown here. However, by the late 1950s all traces had gone and today it is a private residence and offices for a chicken rearing business.

J. Murray of Annan was fortunate to be in the area on 1 August 1906 when this touring car, possibly an Argyll 14-16hp, left the road roughly three miles south east of Kirtlebridge and nosedived into a ditch. Murray was a photographer and he published this shot as a postcard.

Bonshaw tower and house has been the seat of the Irving Clan since the 1300s. The tower is thought to have been built in the second half of the 16th Century, replacing two earlier towers. It was described in 1584 as one of the strongest buildings of the borders. It was altered at a later date with gun loops set into the wall when cannons came into use. The slate roof is of 19th Century construction. The house alongside was built about 1770 for William Irving, Baronet Woodhouse and Robgill. One notable Irving was Sir Robert Irving, a former commodore of the Cunard White Star line and a captain of the RMS *Queen Mary*, who died in 1954. He was noted for docking the Queen Mary in New York without the aid of the normal twelve tugs during a tugmen's strike. The house and tower is now used as a wedding venue.

Bonshaw Mill sat alongside the Kirtle Water on a narrow stretch of land with a steep slope to its rear. The water to power the wheel which in turn powered the machinery came via a mill lade from upstream. Access to the mill was via a steep track which traversed the slope behind the mill building down to the miller's house. Dating from the middle of the 17th Century, it was used to grind oats and wheat. Out of sight behind the mill was a cart shed and granary. The white two-storey building behind was the miller's house. The mill was out of use by 1940 and the wheel and machinery were stripped out, leaving gaping holes where windows, doors and the wheel shaft once were. Some of the original sandstone slabs which once roofed the mill can be seen stacked beside the mill; in recent years a temporary metal roof has been put in place to hold back its dereliction.

Dated 6 April 1906, this photograph shows an overturned wagon lying alongside the main line between Ecclefechan and Kirtlebridge, one of a number of accidents on this stretch of line. It occurred when an express goods train from Glasgow to London, consisting of seventeen wagons and a guards van, derailed from the third wagon onwards, the derailed wagons fouling the other line. Unfortunately this happened just as a passenger train pulling eleven passenger coaches from Carlisle was approaching and, unable to stop in time, it ploughed into the derailed wagons. One passenger on the Carlisle train died and twelve others were injured. The driver and fireman of the passenger train were badly scalded and five others had slight injuries. The official enquiry found that a collapsing wheel had caused the accident and that the speed of the goods train had contributed to the resulting chaos. An earlier accident on this stretch of line in 1872 led to the deaths of eleven passengers and sixteen injured.

Another view of the rail accident at Kirtlebridge on 6 April 1906, showing two rail mounted steam cranes lifting the 4-4-0 engine of the northbound passenger train which ran into the wreckage which had spilled onto the northbound line. Such was the speed of the train that it had no chance of stopping and it rode up over the wreckage and ended up on its side. In the foreground can be seen part of a goods wagon roof, a load of coal spilled from the engine's tender and some of the railway workers standing a safe distance away whilst the lift was in progress.

Opened in 1848, Kirtlebridge Station lay half a mile south of the village. It had an extensive goods yard with narrow gauge lines feeding into it from nearby tile and brickworks, lime quarries and, from 1860, it was the terminus of the Solway line. The yard also had sidings with the facility to use a static crane to load or unload goods. In this view goods wagons and sheeted wagons can be seen in the sidings to the right waiting to be unloaded. In the centre behind the solitary signal can be seen the goods shed. On the left lie more sidings including the connecting branch of the Solway line which merged with the main line. In the distance can be seen the footbridge and the signal box beyond.

Looking northwards up the line at Kirtlebridge Station, some time after 1923 when the London Midland and Scottish Railway came into being. Note the cast iron fountain affixed to the wall of the ticket office and waiting room. To the left of the waiting room can be seen bare ground where spur lines had been lifted. Behind that is the signal box with the other platform across the line to the right-hand side with further station buildings out of picture opposite the signal box. In the distance can be seen the bridge carrying the Brydekirk to Eaglesfield road (B722).

Another view of Kirtlebridge Station, this time looking southwards down the line towards Kirkpatrick Fleming. Taken about 1930, the bushes on the platform have now grown much taller and partially obscure the station buildings on the left. Like most of the stations it closed in 1960 and was demolished shortly thereafter. Now modern housing has encroached into the area to the left of this view.

This view taken at Kirtlebridge looks north across the fields to the main line with the railway cottages (actually a single house which housed railway workers) to the right at the west end of the nine-arch railway viaduct just out of picture. On the left beyond the line lies a line of cottages which included Andrew Calvert's smithy and forge. Above these can be seen the back of the old Kirtle Inn with Braes Farm in the distance. The railway cottages have been demolished and two bungalows now occupy the site, while the smithy is now privately owned and council houses have been built to the left of the inn and down to the cottages.

Eaglesfield lies to the north of Kirtlebridge and boasts the longest village main street in the south of Scotland. Some old cottages spread out along Main Street, leading eventually to the 'big house' (Springkell House), date back to the 18th Century. Interspersed in gaps and clusters can be found substantial red sandstone villas built in the 19th Century. This view from about 1905 looks east. To the immediate right is the shop of J. & W. Nelson, grocers and drapers, with sacks and a sack-barrow standing outside the shop. The cottage beyond was called Thorlaw and the mission hall was located to its rear. Beyond that is Burnswark House which housed Urquhart's shop, which initially was a drapery shop but went on to make up livery costumes for mansion house servants, continuing to do so well into the 19th Century. Across the street are the two sandstone cottages (Myrtle Cottages). Thorlaw cottage and the mission hall were demolished in the 1950s to make way for Eaglesfield's church which is still in use today.

A view of Main Street, Eaglesfield, from about 1910. Up until the 1930s pony and traps and farm carts were the normal forms of transport for the minor gentry, local farmers and tradesmen; poorer locals had to walk or cycle to get around. It was only the well-to-do gentry who could afford cars. On the left is the front of Dunloe Terrace with its clock mounted on its front wall and with Donaldson's shop on the ground floor. Adjoining that is Eaglesfield House with its distinctive bow windows with their fancy parapet edging. On the immediate right behind the hedge is the gable of the village hall, built in 1892 and still in use today. The trees have now gone and gaps between buildings have either council houses or modern buildings filling them.

To celebrate the coronation of King George VI, Eaglesfield, like communities all around the country, created a bonfire to be lit on 22 June 1911 at 10.30 p.m. to commemorate the occasion. A government committee of over 100 lords and MPs had produced a guidance leaflet on building a bonfire to a Boy Scout association design. The community's answer was to build this one which would have taken an incredible effort on the part of the villagers. As can be seen here, the bonfire consisted of a framework of timbers stood on end. Each of the four uprights was made up of two trimmed pine trees lashed together in the middle and set into the ground. Secured by guy ropes they were allowed to slope inwards like a pyramid. Cross planks were then spiked in place, stabilising the structure, and the space in between was then stuffed with cut branches and other timbers all the way up to the top. The ladders were each about 20 feet long and two lashed together allowed a height of about 45 feet for the bonfire. With no mobile cranes at that time, the only power available to hoist the timber into place was horsepower with ropes to steady the timbers until the cross planks were in place. The bonfire would have been visible for miles around, displaying for all to see the patriotism of the community.

In this scene looking west along Eaglesfield's Main Street about 1915 the loaded farm carts were possibly coming from the nearby railway station at Kirtlebridge with goods for the shops, or from the mill with flour or oats. To their left is the whitewashed Thorlaw cottage and beyond that the two-storey Netherby Terrace which housed Nelson's shop. On the right-hand side are Myrtle cottages with the single-storey Lea cottage just beyond. Thorlaw cottage is now gone, replaced in 1953 by the new church, and Netherby Terrace now comprises residential flats.

A cluster of school children standing by Lochaber cottage on Eaglesfield's Main Street. The cottage was the home and working premises of James Rae & Sons, monumental sculptors, a business established in 1883. A number of gravestones are on display in the front yard. The founder, James Rae, had three sons, Orlando, George and William, who followed him in the business. In 1906 the two elder sons moved to Annan and William stayed at Eaglesfield with his father. When he died in 1920 the sons carved the impressive memorial figure from Yorkshire stone which adorns his grave in Middlebie graveyard. The Eaglesfield yard closed in the 1930s and combined with the Annan works which is still in existence today.

Roughly one third of the way along Main Street, at the top of the hill, stood Brecon House cottage on the north side of the street. It was the home of Donaldson's garage in the 1920s with its petrol pump standing just behind the fence. An earlier garage of theirs had been a timber building situated behind their shop elsewhere on Main Street. Next to it is Auricaria cottage which took the name from the two Monkey Puzzle trees on the left; the cottage had belonged to a local worthy called Mrs Rae from about 1905. Today no trace can be seen of the petrol pump or the trees.

On the left of this view of Eaglesfield's Main Street is Oaklea villa, followed by Urquhart's cottage and Mooiplas villa close to the children. On the right in the foreground is Urquhart's shop with the front of Braemar villa just projecting out in front beyond. The car may have belonged to the Carlyle family from Waterbeck or the Johnstone-Fergusons of Springkell House nearby.

EAGLESFIELD HOUSE

Built in 1907 this substantial house was built for Eaglesfield Smith who owned the Eaglesfield estate and for whom the village was named. With its roofs at right angles to the road and with eagle finials at the peaks, it was a distinctive building. Note the old cast-iron drinking fountain tucked in beside the hedge. Taken in the 1930s, this view shows a lorry being loaded with orders for the delivery of goods from Archibald and A.V. Anderson's drapery business with another lorry waiting to be loaded. From the 1930s to the 1970s the business supplied clothing to small shops throughout Scotland and also livery to the large houses, ordered through their travelling salesmen. Adjoining the house is Dunloe Terrace with its clock face on the front wall. It is virtually the same today, except the castellated side extension and the fountain have gone.

Replacing an older school, this one was built in 1908 to a design by architect Frank Carruthers of Dumfries. The builders were Messrs James Rae of Annan and the cost was around £4,000. There was no formal opening with the children simply moving from one building to the other. A distinctive building with its cupola capped ventilation tower, it fronts onto Eaglesfield Main Street. It was modernised in the 1960s and this work included replacing outdoor toilets with indoor toilets and providing new cloakrooms. It was during these renovations that the ventilation tower was removed. More refurbishment was done in 1994/95, the school being extended and updated at a cost of £500,000.

A class at Eaglesfield school. A familiar experience for all of us, as schoolboys and girls the annual class photo always signified that the holidays were near. The downside was that we were warned to stay clean and tidy all day, or else! With parents' backgrounds and incomes varying, the pupils' clothing reflected this while the teachers had the headache of making the class look good; this usually meant putting the smartest looking pupils in the most visible positions and the scruffiest to the back or middle.

Taken in the 1940s, this view shows Kirkpatrick's shop with its proprietor, Tom Kirkpatrick, on the right outside his premises opposite the junction for the Waterbeck road. Leaning up against the wall are three bicycles which would have been the more common form of transport at this time, although in the background can be seen a fine example of a post-war car, possibly a Wolsley. The electricity posts were erected in the early 1930s when most of rural Dumfriesshire was added to the grid. Today the scene has hardly changed apart from the addition of a mobility ramp. The shop is now a post office and grocery called Eaglesfield stores and run by Joanne Strong. It is the only shop in the village.

At the far eastern edge of Eaglesfield lies the hamlet of Sunnybrae which dates back to the eighteenth century. In this view from about 1900, looking back towards the village, the smithy of Andrew Calvert can be seen with its central door wide open and an anvil sitting at the roadside. It was a busy community at this time, home to a tanner with the tan pits lying behind the cottages beyond the smithy. There was also George Armstrong, clogger, Robert Irving, boot and shoemaker, and Isabella Green, grocer. The hamlet has since expanded westwards to join with Eaglesfield.

Springkell House dates from 1734 when it was built for Sir William Maxwell, Baron of Kirkconnel and Springkell. A Palladian-style house, it was built close to the old tower and nearby Kirkconnel church and the Maxwell family graveyard. Between the years 1818 and 1830 Sir John Heron-Maxwell added the wings to either side of the house. The result was said to be a monument to overbuilding. In 1894 the estate was up for sale and was sold to Sir Jabez Johnstone (who later changed this to Johnstone-Ferguson), an industrialist with interests in mining and iron. Shortly thereafter Sir Jabez inherited the Barony of Wiston in Lanarkshire with its estate of roughly 2,000 acres. Over the next decade he undertook extensive remodelling of the interior of Springkell using timber from his estates. It may be that the expense of these undertakings explains the gradual selling off of the farms and grounds of the Wiston estate which today have no connection with Springkell. The medieval churchyard and church (a ruin) near Springkell house the family vault of the Johnstone-Ferguson family. Briefly in the 1940s Springkell was a Barnardo's war evacuation centre. Still in family ownership, it is now run as a hotel and wedding centre.

Newton lies between Kirtlebridge and Kirkpatrick Fleming and this view of its west end was taken in the 1940s looking westwards. The small cottage second from the left housed a barber's shop belonging to David Dunnigan and his wife who also had a sweetie shop here at this time; local resident Elizabeth Moffat recalls being given sweets by Mrs Dunnigan for sitting quietly while her dad had his hair cut. The taller roofs in the middle distance belong to that of Jean Craig's grocery shop and tearoom at the gable end of Victoria Terrace. Beyond the lone cyclist on the right can be seen Lyne Croft private hotel. Later, Jean Craig also opened a bed and breakfast here and often young couples waiting to marry at Gretna stayed here. She also set up a caravan park close to the village.

This photograph taken from in front of Dunnigan's barber shop dates from later in the 1940s. On the left are Jean Craig's grocer's, tearoom and B&B. Beyond that can be seen the frontage of Victoria Terrace, locally known as 'The Hamper' (possibly because it originally comprised 100 'room and kitchens'). It was built in the 1890s to house workers from nearby Cove sandstone quarry. By 1920 there were approximately 50 room and kitchen apartments in the building. These were of a better standard than the old farm cottages nearby but it wasn't until 1931 when the council took over the Terrace and reduced the number of houses here by rearranging the layout of the rooms. Across the road lies the Lyne Croft private hotel. Note that there is now a pavement on one side of the road and an early high topped Albion lorry can be seen on the road. The road has been officially known as the A74 since the 1930s and when the dual carriageway was built in the 1970s, bypassing the village, local passing trade declined.

NEWTON, KIRKPATRICK FLEMING. KF 6.

This late 1930s view of Newton's west end looks along the main road towards Kirkpatrick Fleming. On the immediate left the men are gathered outside Johnston's garage with its petrol pump beside the telegraph pole. The business was set up by David Johnston for his brother's transport company, partly in order to secure a steady supply of fuel in times of shortages. By the 1930s cars were becoming more common and two can be seen here. The trees behind the parked cars have long gone and modern bungalows have replaced them. The transport firm relocated in the 1980s and the garage is now a private house. On the extreme right the roof of Newton Farm can just be seen.

Looking east along the Carlisle road, this view from the early 1900s shows the Station Hotel at the Smithfield end of Kirkpatrick Fleming. The hotel was opened by the Caledonian Railway in the late 19th Century to cater for prospective rail passengers. Between the hotel and the cottages on the left is the road that led to the poorhouse. The row of whitewashed cottages housed the grocer's shop of George Moffat who can be seen with his white apron standing outside the shop near to the water standpipe in the forecourt. As business expanded George started selling bicycles and repairing them; from this it was a short jump to selling petrol and repairing cars. On the original Telford road the garage was well placed to sell petrol as it was the first garage after Carlisle. Both the shop and the garage are still in business today. The village's Victoria Halls can be seen in the background. Just beyond the cart outside Graham's smithy on the right is the start of the road leading down to the station. The trees have now gone and a 1930s council housing scheme has replaced them. Station Road now only leads to a small rail maintenance yard.

In 1851 a joint meeting was held by the parishes of Kirkpatrick Fleming, Dornock, Middlebie, Hoddom, Half Morton and Graitney (Gretna) to discuss the setting up of a combination poorhouse to cover the needs of the area. A site to the north of Kirkpatrick Fleming was selected and John Hodgson, a Carlisle architect, was nominated to carry out the work. The final building was T-shaped, two storeys high, designed to house over 100 inmates, and completed in 1863. The main entrance shown in the centre of this view from about 1910 led into a hall with the master's rooms and the entrances to the male and female quarters. The short leg of the T at the rear contained a chapel cum dining room with a basement below. The basement comprised a reception room with two baths, store rooms and a men's dayroom. In the other half were the kitchen, larder, scullery and laundry room. The men and women slept on the first floor in separate dormitories on palliases stuffed with straw. They had separate yards for exercise and toilets in those yards for their use. By 1922 it was renamed the Notwen Combination Poorhouse and in the 1930s Notwen House. It continued to offer council-run housing until the 1960s when it became a home for the elderly, which it still is today.

Looking north into Kirkpatrick Fleming Station yard about 1920, a south-bound passenger train stands at the platform. On the left in front of the trees the signal box which controlled the line and the sidings is just visible. Alongside the stationary train is a goods train with goods being unloaded into lorries for onward delivery. The siding to the immediate right led into another loading area with a stationary seven ton capacity crane for unloading or loading heavy goods. Cut sandstone from the nearby Cove quarry was shipped out from this station until the quarry closed in the 1920s. The station closed in 1960 and was demolished shortly thereafter. The site is now a small maintenance yard but as late as 2010 the ruin of the old ticket office was still in evidence.

This view of Kirkpatrick Fleming from the 1930s looks west towards Kirtlebridge. On the immediate right stands the Victoria Public Hall, built in 1898. An unusual feature of the hall is that it has two halls, one large and one small. It was extensively used by the local community for dances, weddings and other functions and obviously had a licence as there are two beer barrels sitting at the verge. Beyond that is Moffat's garage and shop; three generations of the family have run both to the present day. George Moffat started the shop about 1905 and also sold, hired and repaired bicycles. The building just beyond is the Station Hotel. Over the years this has had a number of owners and is still in business today. The hall is now looked after by a community group and a bungalow occupies the space between it and the garage and shop.

One of many hamlets in this area, Chapelknowe stands to the north east of Kirkpatrick Fleming on the B6357 road to Canonbie. It has a 12th Century origin and contained a medieval church with ties to Robert the Bruce and Guisborough Priory. It was sometimes also known as Timpanheck as was its church. Since this photograph was taken it has expanded with new houses built mainly for people commuting to towns further afield.

The church shown here about 1910 was built in the mid-18th Century with various alterations and renovations made in 1889 by the architect George Dale Oliver. These alterations included the tall lancet windows, the unusual tower roof vent and the battlemented birdcage belfry. It was built to the north of Chapelknowe on the site of the much earlier medieval church. Like its predecessor, it was called Timpanheck but is better known as Half-Morton church after the old parish name. Since 1992 it has been a private dwelling and the nearest church still in use is that of Kirkpatrick Fleming which holds one service every month.

This view from the 1950s looks down the main street (now B6357) of the hamlet of Hollee which lies to the south west of Kirkpatrick Fleming on the Annan road. The hamlet is one of many in this area dating back to the mid-18th Century and would initially have been known as a fermtoun, built to house estate or farm workers. The houses would have originally been built of clay daub with stone floors and thatched roofs, but as estates needed to attract workers they had to upgrade the accommodation accordingly. Hollee was also known locally as 'the fairy ra' (row) but it is not known why, although among the older generation the description is still in use. The lane on the right accessed the backs of the houses to allow the removal of waste from outside toilets before the advent of inside toilets and still allows access today.

Irvington is another hamlet between Hollee and the south of Kirtlebridge. It is typical of late-19th Century rural estate buildings, built to house workers. Landowners placed these clusters of buildings strategically around their estates so that no time was wasted for the occupants in getting to work. As most landowners had put in the original roads across their estates they could and did dictate where bus routes would go by the placement of these hamlets. Housing on a bus route also made it easier to attract farm workers.